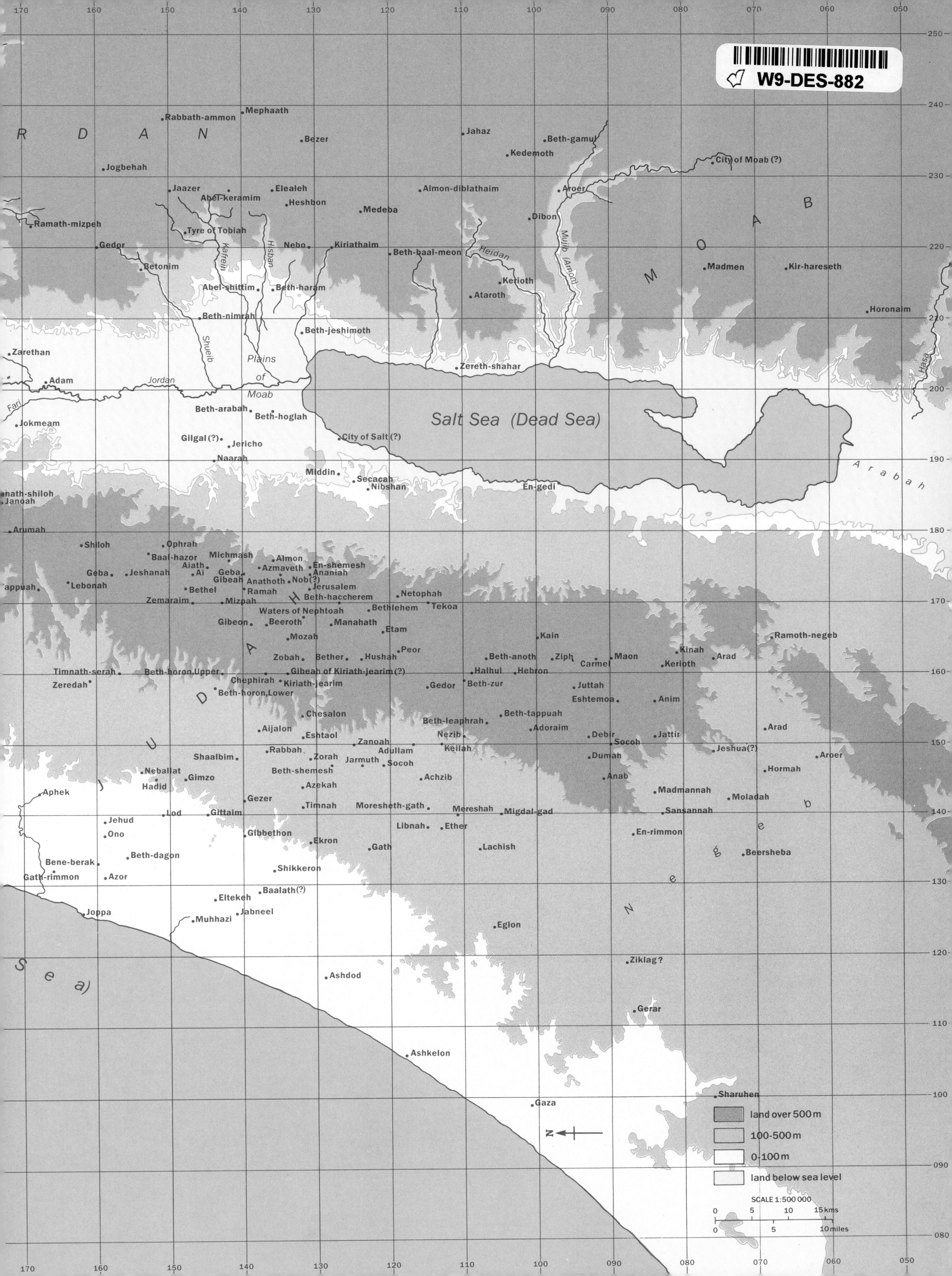

R D A N
M O A B
J U D A H
N e g e b
S e a)
Salt Sea (Dead Sea)
Plains of Moab
Arabah
Jordan
Fari
Shueib
Kafrein
Hisban
Heidan
Mujib (Arnon)
Hasa
Rabbath-ammon
Mephaath
Bezer
Jahaz
Beth-gamul
Kedemoth
City of Moab (?)
Jogbehah
Jaazer
Abel-keramim
Elealeh
Heshbon
Almon-diblathaim
Aroer
Medeba
Dibon
Ramath-mizpeh
Tyre of Tobiah
Gedor
Nebo
Kiriathaim
Beth-baal-meon
Betonim
Madmen
Kir-hareseth
Kerioth
Abel-shittim
Beth-haram
Ataroth
Beth-nimrah
Horonaim
Beth-jeshimoth
Zarethan
Zereth-shahar
Adam
Beth-arabah
Beth-hoglah
Jokmeam
Gilgal (?)
Jericho
City of Salt (?)
Naarah
Middin
Secacah
Nibshan
En-gedi
nath-shiloh
Janoah
Arumah
Shiloh
Ophrah
Baal-hazor
Michmash
Almon
En-shemesh
Aiath
Ai
Geba
Azmaveth
Ananiah
Geba
Jeshanah
Gibeah
Anathoth
Nob (?)
appuah
Lebonah
Bethel
Ramah
Jerusalem
Netophah
Zemaraim
Mizpah
Beth-haccherem
Tekoa
Waters of Nephtoah
Bethlehem
Gibeon
Beeroth
Manahath
Etam
Mozah
Kain
Ramoth-negeb
Peor
Zobah
Bether
Hushah
Beth-anoth
Ziph
Carmel
Maon
Kinah
Arad
Kerioth
Timnath-serah
Beth-horon,Upper
Gibeah of Kiriath-jearim (?)
Halhul
Hebron
Zeredah
Chephirah
Kiriath-jearim
Gedor
Beth-zur
Juttah
Beth-horon,Lower
Eshtemoa
Anim
Chesalon
Beth-tappuah
Beth-leaphrah
Adoraim
Aijalon
Eshtaol
Nezib
Debir
Jattir
Arad
Zanoah
Socoh
Shaalbim
Rabbah
Adullam
Keilah
Jeshua (?)
Zorah
Jarmuth
Socoh
Dumah
Aroer
Neballat
Beth-shemesh
Hormah
Hadid
Gimzo
Achzib
Anab
Aphek
Azekah
Madmannah
Gezer
Moladah
Timnah
Moresheth-gath
Mereshah
Lod
Gittaim
Migdal-gad
Sansannah
Jehud
Libnah
Ether
Ono
Gibbethon
En-rimmon
Ekron
Beth-dagon
Gath
Lachish
Beersheba
Bene-berak
Shikkeron
Gath-rimmon
Azor
Baalath (?)
Eltekeh
Joppa
Jabneel
Muhhazi
Eglon
Ziklag ?
Ashdod
Gerar
Ashkelon
Sharuhen
Gaza
N
land over 500 m
100-500 m
0-100 m
land below sea level
SCALE 1:500 000
0 5 10 15 kms
0 5 10 miles
170 160 150 140 130 120 110 100 090 080 070 060 050
250 240 230 220 210 200 190 180 170 160 150 140 130 120 110 100 090 080

HarperCollins

ATLAS OF THE BIBLE